Usborne

Fairy Ponies Colouring Book

Contents

Illustrated by Barbara Bongini

Designed by Brenda Cole

Written by Lesley Sims and Zanna Davidson

Holly and the Fairy Ponies

Meet Holly and her friends. Holly has discovered a magical world...
Hidden inside the old oak tree, at the bottom of her
great-aunt's garden, she found wonderful
Pony Island where fairy ponies live.

Holly

To enter Pony Island, Holly
sprinkles herself with magic dust.
Rainbow sparkles surround her and
she shrinks to the size of a fairy.

Puck

Holly's best friend on Pony
Island. He's a brave little pony
and always eager for
an adventure.

Dandelion

Puck's friend. Another young
fairy pony, friendly and
mischievous, she likes playing
tricks on Puck.

Pony Queen

The noble, powerful ruler
of Pony Island. Butterflies
flutter around her
wherever she goes.

Bluebell

Puck's mother and one of Pony Island's
Spell Keepers, the most magical and
important ponies on the island. She has a
gleaming coat and a long flowing mane.

Princess Rosabel

The Pony Queen's niece. She lives on nearby Waterfall Island, across the Rainbow Sea.

Spray

A river pony who lives in the Singing River. His body is pearly green and his eyes are ocean blue.

Dancer

Puck's uncle and another Spell Keeper, dedicated to protecting Pony Island. He's ready to fly to the rescue at a moment's notice.

Izagard

A wise old wizard pony, who lives in a cottage in the High Mountains. He has a silvery coat and an icy white mane.

Willow

One of the unicorns who lives on Pony Island in the Enchanted Wood.

Shadow

An evil pony who has turned against the Pony Queen and wants to rule Pony Island himself.

3

Fairy Pony Island

Unicorn Prince's Palace

Home of the Unicorn Prince, ruler of the unicorns who live on Pony Island. The palace's golden gates are hidden from strangers behind enchanted vines.

Pony Magic School

Where young fairy ponies go to learn magic, memorising spells and studying all the legends that surround the island.

Magic Pony Pools

Sparkling pools with amazing healing powers. Visited by the Pony Queen every day for her Royal Bath Time.

Dark Forest

Lake of Gilded Lilies

Dancing Waterfall

Unicorn Prince's Palace

Enchanted Wood

Pony Magic School

Magic Pony Pools

Woody Glade

Sunlit Sea

High
Mountains

Izagard's House

Izagard's House

A snug cottage in the High
Mountains, filled with
books of magic
and folklore.

Everlasting
Rainbow

Summer
Palace

Rainbow
Mountain

Summer Palace

The elegant home
of the Pony Queen.
Built of gleaming
white marble, it
houses the Necklace
of Wishes which can
grant the wearer's
deepest desire.

Forever
Flower Meadow

Rainbow
Shore

Butterfly
Valley

Silver Stream

Singing River

Home of the river
ponies, who are
summoned by
whistling a
special tune.

Singing River

Meadows

Entrance from
the Great Oak

N
W   E
S

The Welcome Ceremony

On Holly's first visit, she makes a promise never to tell where the fairy ponies dwell. The Pony Queen gives her a silver bell to ring whenever she wants to return. Then ponies fill the sky, showering her with flowers.

6

Picnic by the Singing River

The banks of the Singing River are the perfect spot for a picnic.
Bluebell and Dancer join Holly, Puck and Dandelion enjoying
luscious peaches, dewberries and sticky honeycakes.

Flying over Pony Island

Holly and Puck soar over Pony Island, as it sparkles in the sunshine. The Everlasting Rainbow shimmers behind them and the island is a glorious sight of shining purples, golden yellows and emerald greens.

Magic Pony Pools

Every day, the fairy ponies visit the Magic Pony Pools to splash and play and bathe. The rippling water fills them with a sense of well-being and boosts their magical powers.

Spell Keepers' Parade

Holly waves to the Spell Keepers as they follow the Pony Queen in a majestic flying parade. Bays, roans, palominos and ponies with glossy chestnut coats fly faster than the wind on their iridescent butterfly wings.

Inside the Summer Palace

Holly and Puck are exploring the Pony Queen's palace.
A glittering chandelier flashes rainbow reflections around
the room, lighting up paintings and statues.

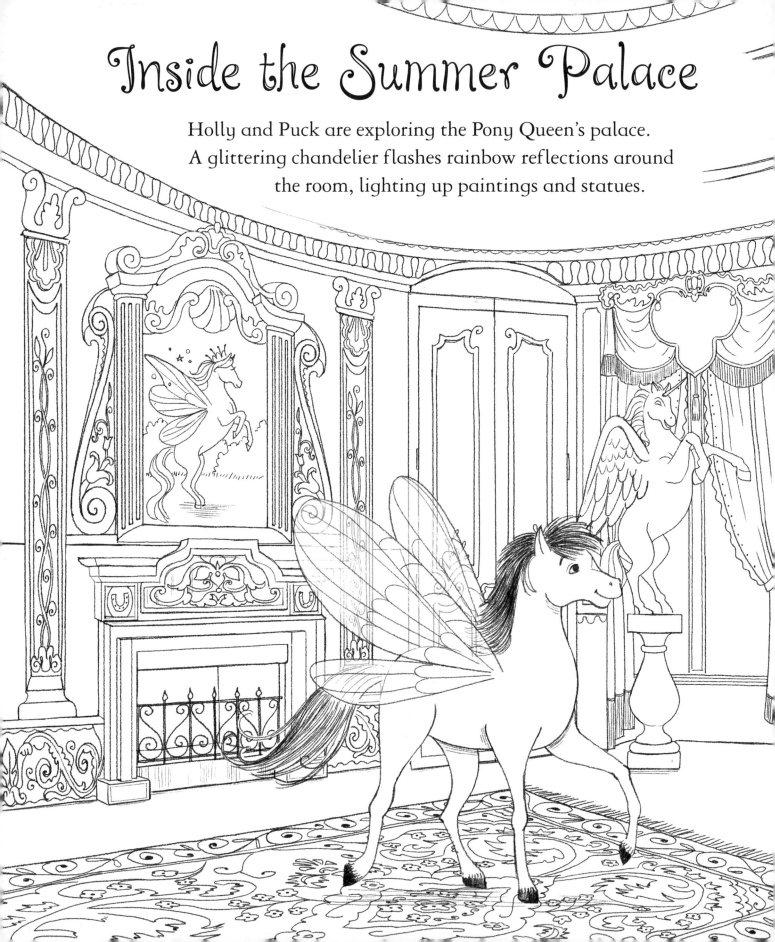

Unicorn Garden

Willow is showing Holly and Puck around the beautiful gardens of the Unicorn Prince's Palace. Exotic flowers fill the air with their fragrant scent and a fountain splashes bright pink waterlilies with glistening drops of water.

Stopping Shadow

Hidden deep in the Dark Forest, Holly, Puck and Princess Rosabel have stumbled on Shadow and his henchmen. While they are caught up in their wicked plot, the fairy ponies cast a spell. Blazing fireworks fizz and pop around them, stopping Shadow and his friends in their tracks.

River Pony

Puck and Dandelion are summoning Spray to introduce Holly.
As Puck whistles a tuneful melody, the Singing River bubbles
and gurgles and Spray bursts out of the water, beating
his glittering dragonfly wings.

23

Rainbow Races

Holly and Puck are competing in the Rainbow Races, the biggest event on Pony Island. Gaily painted rainbow masts mark the start of an obstacle course – but who will be the first pony to fly through the rainbow?

Dancing Waterfall

On a hot sunny day, everyone comes to the Dancing Waterfall to fly through its crystal blue water and keep cool. Dazzling butterflies flit by Holly, as she weaves a satin-soft flower necklace for Puck.

Enchanted Wood

Deep in the Enchanted Wood, Holly and Puck are playing
hide-and-seek with Willow the unicorn and her friends.
Holly darts in and out between tall, graceful trees, their
trunks shining with a silvery bark.

29

Tea with Izagard

Snowflakes whirl outside Izagard's cottage as the wizard pony hosts
a tea party. A merrily burning fire fills the room with a rosy glow.
Toasted marshmallows melt over the flames, while a bowl of golden
honey mead warms Holly to her toes.

Good Night

It's time for Holly to head home to her great-aunt's
cottage and bed. Puck flies her back over a sleeping
Pony Island, through a starry, moonlit sky.

Based on the **Young Reading Fairy Ponies** series, part of the **Usborne Reading Programme**.
First published in 2015 by Usborne Publishing Ltd, Usborne House, 83-85 Saffron Hill, London EC1N 8RT, England.
www.usborne.com Copyright © 2015 Usborne Publishing Ltd. The name Usborne and the devices ⊕ ♀ are Trade Marks of Usborne
Publishing Ltd.